# How to Talk to Anyone with Power and Confidence

*The Step by Step Guide to Learn How to Communicate Effectively and Efficiently*

## Rock H. Bankole

*With Cheryl J. Jerabek*

# Digital Print House

## BE A BETTER YOU

# Acknowledgments

I would like to recognize, acknowledge, and applaud all the people around the world that helped make this book and this mission possible. I cannot name you one by one; but you know who you are. I am honored to serve with you on this noble mission of educating the world and helping each individual in becoming a better person today than he was yesterday.

I would like to specifically highlight and mention those individuals who were directly instrumental in the writing and publishing of this book: Yola Angeline Alonzo, Minerva Buenaluz, Cheryl Green, and Daryl Corilla.

# YOUR FREE BONUS

## Download another Book for Free

I want to thank you for buying this book. Our hope is to assist you even further in your quest of developing powerful self-confidence by giving you the captivating confidence workbook for free.

Click the link below to receive it:

http://www.imreadytoshine.com/confidence-workbook

This is a very comprehensible and step-by-step quick-start guide with printable sheet that will help you build your Confidence.

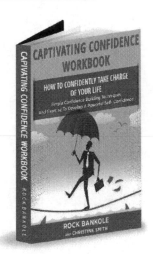

In addition to getting this workbook, you will also have the opportunity to get my new books for free, and receive other valuable emails that will help you.

Again, here is the link to get your free workbook.

http://www.imreadytoshine.com/confidence-workbook

# Contents

# Introduction

Are you one of those people who just walks into a room and everyone drops what they are doing to hear what you have to say? Don't worry. I wasn't either, but I taught myself to talk effectively and I'll teach you, too.

Chances are, if you are reading this book, your communication skills can use some improvement. You talk and no one listens; chances are, they don't even realize you are talking.

The time has come that not being heard is no longer working for you. You have the job of a lifetime that hinges on an awesome interview. You have been selected to present a career changing strategy to your boss. Or, perhaps you are in a relationship that you want to last but your lack of communication skills is jeopardizing it. You're in luck! That's exactly what you're about to learn...how to communicate so people will listen and truly hear you.

I was the world's worst communicator. I suffered from severe panic attacks when I did any type of public speaking. The first one happened when I had to give a speech in ninth grade. I was so nervous, I almost passed out. Every time thereafter that I spoke in front of a group, it was an instant replay. Instead of hearing, "Great speech", I heard words of comfort like, "I just wanted to get up on the stage and give you a hug." Uhm...not the response I was looking for.

I was even worse face-to-face. I just rattled on and had no real direction with any conversation. I had no idea what I was trying to say, so neither did anyone else. I might as well have been a wallflower. No one heard me anyway and…it was my own fault.

I was missing out on life… and so are you. I took matters into my own hands and taught myself to speak to anyone and not just to speak, but to communicate effectively. I taught the most difficult student ever-- myself. I will teach you, too.

Do you get intimidated when you talk to people in power, like your boss? I did, too. Do you write better than you talk, or do better listening rather than joining in a conversation? Does your lack of communication skills hold you back? In this book, you are going to learn what to do about these weaknesses.

Perhaps you don't have a devastating communication breakdown issue like I had. Maybe your skills are "good enough." How is that working for you? I am a firm believer that generally in life, *good enough* is never…good enough. And when it comes to communication, which is the key to practically everything in life, settling with just *good enough* is a sad way to live. Here's your challenge to rise above and beyond your weaknesses and to take charge so you can communicate your way to the top. Talk about power!

When you can effectively communicate and talk to anyone, you can own your life again. You are not at the random mercy of just accepting the assumption that you cannot talk well. Grab the bull by the horns and change your entire life. Get that job. Take your career to the next level. Get that girl (or guy) and keep her (or him). Get what you want and do it with confidence and charisma.

You will be at the helm. You will be the driver when you learn to talk and truly communicate with confidence.

It may sound like a tall order, but remember, I was also the worst talker ever. But, I reached the pits of despair because of my inability. It was a handicap that I didn't have to have--one that I could steer through...if I only had the courage and determination. Fortunately, I did.

You too can break the barriers of communication. You can become an expert in talking, listening and having genuine, productive communication skills that will change your life forever.

Don't put it off another day. Chances are you've gone through a lifetime of not being able to effectively communicate. You see where that has gotten you. Well, by reading this book, you are about to take a giant step forward into a whole new life. Trust me. You'll wonder why you waited as long as you did. Without further ado, let's get started so you can learn effective communication skills...today!

# Chapter 1

# To Talk Well, You Must Know People Well

You probably know the feeling. An important person comes up to you -- someone you look up to, maybe your boss, a politician or a pastor. Your heart races. You can't believe he is giving you the time of day. "How's the wife and kids?" he asks. Your world crumbles. You...have no wife and kids.

It doesn't have to be someone important who is speaking to us to make us feel important...or not. Even the person sitting next to us on the bus has the ability to make us feel significant, or, like we don't matter at all. Regardless of how we may try to wiggle around it, while the ultimate goal of your communication may be to inform or express, you are never going to succeed at doing so if the person you are talking to feels you have no value for him or her. If you think about it, your reaction is, no doubt, the same.

After that "important person" greeted you and got up to give his speech or sermon, did you want to listen to it? Every (good) speaker knows that the best delivery is one that makes each person in the audience feel every word was just for him or her. If the speaker bombed out when speaking to you one-on-one, chances are his speech was a bomb in your book as well. Why? You did not feel significant. You didn't matter to him and therefore, his matters don't matter to you either.

In the art of effective conversation as well as public speaking, it is imperative to take an interest in the person or persons you are talking to. Know what they like and what they don't like. Learn what interests them. Above all, don't ask about their wife and kids if they don't have any. Do your homework and you'll ace the test!

## Three Basic Hungers Every Person Has in Common

People all over the world are so different. We walk, talk, t and think differently. That is what makes us individuals; and it would be a very drab world if this weren't true. Because we are all so different, finding something in common with another person or group becomes exciting. When we have something in common with the majority of everyone else in the world, it gets even more exciting.

There are three basic things that all people crave for. They can't get enough of it and suffer if they don't get their fill. Let's take a look at these three needs.

### 1 - Acceptance

Before you can accept someone, it's important to grasp the full meaning of the word. Acceptance is to show respect for people as they are. It is a validation that you accept people for who they are, not who you want them to be.

According to Neuropsychologist, Rick Hanson, Ph. D., in an article that appeared on Psychology Today's website entitled "Accept Them as They Are", accepting people doesn't necessarily mean that you agree with or approve of them or their actions. It is not a matter of waiving your own rights or downplaying the impact that person has on you.

Your boss may grate on your nerves. He is overweight, talks too loud and drinks too much, but, aside from his downfalls and regardless of how his actions affect you, you take him as he is and respect him as a person-- although you would like to change a few things about him if given the chance.

On the same token, you are sitting beside a person on the airplane who has political material strewn about. You get the feeling this individual is an important member of the political party you oppose. Still, regardless of your differences, you and he are able to carry on a nice, casual conversation to pass the time on the flight. Why? Because you respect his or her right to be who they are, to like what they like, and believe what they believe. You…accept that person although you certainly don't agree with them, on politics at least.

People have the inborn need to be accepted. It's human nature and was bred into us. Our brain stimulates the need and desire for others to approve of us. The brain is an amazing organ. According to an article written on behalf of The American Psychological Association by Kirsten Weir, the insatiable need to be accepted very well may stem from the primal quest for survival. "Like hunger or thirst," she wrote. "Our need for acceptance emerged as a mechanism for survival." As long as man has been on the earth, he has been dependent on social groups and relationships with other individuals in order to survive. That…has not changed.

Furthermore, psychologically speaking, rejection hurts. Acceptance feels good. The need and desire to bond, connect, and relate to other human beings is built into us. We all need to feel accepted.

Teen-agers get the worst rap for seeking approval. "If she jumped off a cliff, would you jump off a cliff too?" you may recall your mother asking when you and your best buddy got into trouble. The fact is that, especially during the teen years when we are transitioning from being a dependent child to making our own independent choices as adults, the longing to be liked can lead to problems such as peer pressure and so forth. But, it can also have positive effects on us.

One thing is guaranteed. If you try to talk to someone and come across as non-accepting of them, you will get nowhere. Picture an auditorium full of high school students. Their principal is spewing anger and giving them the "what to" in a very long lecture. Do you think the students are all ears and receptive of his message? Probably not so much. If what you are saying to the person you are talking to is not projecting their acceptance, you might as well give it up. Your words are falling on deaf ears; and that is not communication.

On the other hand, if you are showing that you accept the person you are speaking to, there is no end to where the conversation may lead. Just the other day, I was talking to a young man about his dog. I love dogs and respect him as a great pet parent. He could sense that and before I knew it. He was sharing some very personal information and deep feelings about a dog he previously had who died of cancer. The interesting thing is that I don't personally know this young man and I am pretty sure I now know more about him, at least in regards to his deceased dog, than most people who are close to him. I probably know things that his own mother doesn't know about him and his feelings. Why? Because he knew I accepted him, not only as a fellow pet parent, but as a human being as well.

Try talking to someone on an accepting level. Through your tone of voice, body language, eye contact, and certainly through your actual words, you will convey that you respect who they are. You will see how receptive people are to listen and actually take part in a meaningful conversation when you do so.

## 2 - Approval

Here's where it gets tricky. But, don't cave in. If there weren't some tricks in the bag along the way, everyone would know what I am about to teach you.

The difference between a person seeking acceptance and one seeking approval is one who seeks approval often looks for it for the wrong reason and for the wrong thing or things. If an individual is seeking approval in order to feel whole or more secure about himself, he is out of luck. Neither you nor anyone else can satisfy that kind of a need in another human being.

Likewise, if a person is dependent upon others approving of everything he does, that is also wrong. You can love your spouse more than anything under the sun. You love him or her to the moon and back as the saying goes. But do you approve of everything that he or she thinks, does, or feels? I bet not. And if your significant other is looking to have your approval in all those areas, he or she will resort to selling out to a people-pleasing personality, lead a double life, or some other drastic measure will be taken. No one totally pleases anyone. That's a fact!

But human nature does crave approval. And that's alright. It is normal to seek to please. That is, in theory at least, your brain's way of working through your emotions to keep you alive. If you didn't give a flip about what anyone thought, you would probably end up in a whole lot of trouble.

We need people to validate us. We just need to recognize the fact that they are validating us as humans, not necessarily agreeing with every thought we make and each action we take.

My friend's father wanted him to be an attorney. His father was a notorious one and had full intentions of passing on the torch. My friend, however, wanted to be a writer. This didn't set well for years. Finally, one day, his aging father relented to approve of him as an adult who had followed his dreams, gotten educated and diligently worked to succeed within his field of passion. His father approved of his son and even somewhat approved of his diligence (going to school to further his education, hard work, etc.), but he never did approve of his end goal to be a writer, not even when he became a world renowned and an accomplished one.

You can approve of a person yet not approve of everything they do, say or think. And…vice versa. Once you communicate to a person (by any means of communication, both verbal and non-verbal) that you approve of them, you have an audience. You have a receptive listener and participant to the conversation. Take it a step further and actually agree with at least one thing that is important to him or her and you have someone who not only will listen and communicate with you, they will do so eagerly.

## 3 - Appreciation

This one is HUGE! I cannot stress it enough. Some of the best advice I ever got in regard to people is this: Lower your expectation and raise your appreciation. The results are priceless.

To fully understand the concept, think of how you feel when you are appreciated…and when you are not. When was the last time you did something and expected a big "Thank you!" in return but got nil? Chances are you didn't do it just for that reason. You did what you did from your heart. It was a favor, something nice you did just because. But, it's always nice to be appreciated behind your act of good will. When was the last time you went out of your way for that person? If you're like me…it was a while.

I remember being in a setting where team building was the object of the game. We were given the assignment to do something nice for someone but ordered NOT to let that person find out who did it. I enjoyed the task. It made me take a good look at how often we, as humans, do things for recognition or some form of self-satisfaction. It's not wrong to seek appreciation but it is nice, once in a while, to do things without it as a motive at all.

People love to be appreciated. It inspires us to do more. Think of someone you know who really appreciates something you do, give, or don't do. Does your wife tell you all the time that she appreciates your loyalty to her? Does your husband frequently tell you he appreciates all you do for him? Maybe you have a friend who appreciates spending time with you and is quick to let you know as much. Or, maybe you have one particular child who gets super excited when you bring home a surprise for him or her. Being appreciated instigates and motivates us to give more, to do more…to be more.

The next time you talk to someone, let them know you appreciate them. You can do so in many ways, including verbally stating the fact. If your boss is great about letting you off work early to go watch your son play baseball, tell him. Does your best friend listen to endless hours of your woes? Tell her. If the janitor at your church does a good job, say as much. Then, carry on a conversation behind it. You will have the best one ever. Knowing that you are appreciated satisfies a hunger within you, and binds you somehow with the person that has honestly given you appreciation.

## First Impression Always Lasts

Experts tell us that we get mere seconds to make our impression on someone. There is no retake. This is live. No "take 2". It's the real deal and it is instant. But if you are aware of it, you can use it to your advantage. Take matters into your own hands and make a good and lasting first impression.

Psychologists call it being "thin cut". Laymen often refer to it as being "sized up". Whatever you choose to entitle it, opinions about you are made in seconds and you are being judged by these factors:

- Your social status

- Your intelligence

- Your sexual preference (whether gay or straight)

- If you are promiscuous

- If you are adventurous

- Your dominance

- Your trustworthiness

- Your level of success

The good news is that you have the power to choose and project what impression you leave on someone. You can be an instant winner. Dress and act like a lad and no matter how serious you look, people will just treat you like a boychick. On the other hand, look and act like champion, a winner, or a respected fellow and people will treat you as such a man.

You alone decide the way you want people to interact with you, so next time, make sure to look and act as you wish the other person would see and act toward you.

## How to Make the Other Person Feel Important

Another ace you have up your sleeve is that you can make the person you are talking to feel important. Everyone wants to feel important. They want to matter. It is only natural to feel that way.

Right off the bat, you can make the other guy feel important. It is a gift you can give and in return, you can bet you will have his attention. It's a wonderful game of give and take.

Here are some pointers in making people feel important:

13

- Talk about them. People like that. It makes them feel…important.

- Talk about things they are interested in. Take the time to find out what their interests are and research about those things.

- Ask them questions about themselves and things that interest them.

- If you are not sure if they have a family, don't ask how their family is doing.

- Find out any trips or special things they have recently done.

- If they have a hobby, talk about it. If you aren't sure if they do or not, ask them.

- Talk about their achievements if you know of any.

- Be genuine.

- Search for any similar interests the two of you share.

## Everybody's favorite subject is about themselves.

### Use this to your advantage

Later in the book, you will learn all about how people love to talk about themselves. There are some scientific evidences that may surprise you. It's not a bad thing, in fact, it's all good. We were born with the need and desire to talk about ourselves so do whatever is within your means to strike up conversations that center around the person you are speaking with. You are sure to get their attention when you do.

**People Will Feel Your Fear**

I recently attended a graduation where the principal of the school was speaking. He was so nervous, it made me uncomfortable. Having suffered from severe public speaking anxiety myself, I felt his pain. I wanted to go give him a hug and a copy of this book. I took a look around and everyone in the audience looked as if they felt the same way...sorry for him.

When you are uptight about speaking, be it publicly or privately, people sense your fear. While you work on getting over your anxiety of talking through measures taken in this book, you can fake it until you make it. Just pretending that you are not so nervous will help relax the person or persons you are speaking to and it might calm you as well.

## Assume That People Will Like You and They Will.

Dr. Phil McGraw, television talk host and highly accredited psychologist says it like it is. We teach people how to treat us. Over and over again, Dr. Phil reminds his talk show guests of this fact and it will do us good to remind ourselves, too. When we assume that people will like us, (I mean, after all, why wouldn't they?) Then we give them the cue to like us. If we assume that they will not like us, we are, in turn, giving them the signal to not like us. They are aware that we know ourselves best and if we are projecting our own "un-likeability," then there must be a reason. Assume people will like you and they will.

## Chapter Takeaways

1. In order to get to know someone, it is important to learn something about them such as their likes and dislikes.

2. Everyone craves acceptance, approval and appreciation.

3. Treat people with importance. They will sense your respect and listen to you.

4. People love to talk about themselves. Use this fact to your advantage.

5. Assume people will like you and they will.

# Chapter 2

# Can We Talk?

*"To speak and to speak well are two things. A fool may talk, but a wise man speaks."*

-Ben Jonson

The party is loud. People are laughing and having a great time. Glasses are being raised, jokes are being told...but wait. A hush falls over the room. Not a word is spoken. You can hear a pin drop. There is total silence. A man walks in. Everyone stops what they are doing to hear what he has to say. When E.F. Hutton talks...people listen!

You may (or may not) remember the 1970-1980 old-school commercials where financial broker, E.F. Hutton, could walk into any room and everyone immediately stopped whatever they were doing to listen to him. Why? Because he had something to say.

Chances are you have something to say, too. That's why we talk. We talk in order to communicate. We want others to know what we think, how we feel, how to do something or whatever else it is we might need or want to convey.

## What IS Talk?

We can talk the talk or talk or just be talking to the wall. You can talk just to hear yourself talk. We can talk till we're blue in the face, be all talk or no talk at all. There's tall talk, sweet talk, pillow talk, double talk, loose talk and even heart-to-heart talk. Money talks. But, talk can be cheap. That's a lot of talk about talk but what IS talk anyway?

Talking is, by definition, the act of speaking to express ideas or feelings or to inform. Talking is a means of communication. It plays a huge role in human interaction. It serves a myriad of purposes and can bring about positive or negative, results. Talking can make or break our relationships, get us hired…or fired, and ultimately can make our lives better…or worse. Yes, talking is THAT important.

## Can I Have Your Attention Please?

It's a great feeling to be heard. Like E.F. Hutton, you speak…people listen. Likewise, it's a horrible feeling to not be heard or to not be able to start a conversation. Being ignored is one of the most cruel punishments known to mankind. In fact, when I was growing up, I got the silent treatment whenever I got into trouble. I was ignored. I felt I didn't exist. If you have personally experienced the frustration of not being heard when you talk, read on, my friend. I am about to teach you how to get people to listen by getting their attention. Trust me…it's a great feeling!

## Talking vs. Communication

As mentioned before, talk is speaking in order to express an idea or feeling or to give information. Communication, however, is the exchange of information, feeling, or ideas. It is a social interaction. Communication is talking and being heard, felt, and understood.

Whether you are talking to one person or to a group of people, what you are saying is either received or not. If what you are saying is causing a connection with those whom you are talking to, you are communicating. Congratulations! Communication is the key to effective talking.

## Communication vs. Effective Communication

This is where it gets a little tricky, so stay with me. The information I am about to give you makes a world of difference when it comes to truly conveying your message to others, be it information, an idea, or a feeling.

The object of talking is to communicate, that's a given. But even though you communicate, or make a connection through your words, that still doesn't guarantee the results you are looking for. Effective communication gets results.

Maybe you are giving a speech for a fund raising event. Not only do you want to tell the group about the cause, you want to reach the ultimate goal of raising money. What you say needs to stir up something inside your audience that would encourage them to give. That's when effective communication comes in. When you effectively communicate, you provoke emotions and action. Your words command results.

## The Art of Communication

Effective communication is an art. You need to express yourself creatively and skillfully. Many people make their living through the art of talking and expression. Many of these are actors and actresses, motivational speakers, and even salesmen and saleswomen.

For those of us who struggle to get through an average conversation and completely panic at the thought of giving a speech or going through a job interview, it can be hard to imagine being so good at talking, not to mention, even making a career out of it. But many do; and by the end of this book, you can, too. Even if you don't want to build your entire career around talking, mastering the art of communication will still greatly improve many areas of your life including your relationships with your significant other, your children, friends, your boss, co-workers, and even clients and customers.

You might just get a few frills with the deal too. Those with good social skills tend to gain favor with others. They get better jobs, better results with clients, and tend to be happier people all the way around.

## Interesting Facts about Talking

- Women talk three times as much as men.

- It has been proven that those who talk to themselves have a higher IQ.

- Communication is 93% non-verbal (more on that subject later!).

## Chapter Takeaways

1. Talking is a method of communication, but it is not complete communication.

2. Communication is a two-way street.

3. There are many factors, physical and mental, that go along with good communication.

4. You can improve the way you communicate with others.

5. Women talk more than men.

# Chapter 3

# Talk to Me!

*"Can you hear me now?"*

\- Verizon

## What Are You Trying to Say?

You've heard it before, more times than you probably cared to. Someone is talking and you have no clue to what they are really saying. You get the distinct impression that they don't know what they are trying to say either.

The art of communication begins with defining the purpose of what you have to say. It doesn't need to be a big announcement or anything of significant importance. You may just be conversing with a friend about how your morning went or about a sale at the grocery store. Even still, it is imperative that you identify the idea, information, or feeling that you are trying to express because if you do not know what it is you are trying to say, it is a given that no one else will either.

## What are Your Expectations?

Often enough, people enter a conversation without knowing what it is they are trying to accomplish. What are their goals and how would they know that the conversation was successful?

If you are trying to befriend someone, your attitude should radically be different from how you should behave if you are trying to sell something to someone or build a meaningful relationship with other people. It is important to know why you are starting the conversation in the first place. How would you know that you have succeeded?

Once you have identified what you wish to say and what purpose you have for saying it, it's time to get talking. Let's get down to business and apply some very valuable techniques you are going to learn in this book so that you will not only talk but truly communicate and do so with confidence and power. Ready?

## The Importance of Small Talk - How to Start a Conversation With a Push of a Button

The sound of silence. Sometimes silence is golden. Other times it is awkward. For those that are not naturally blessed with the gift of gab, starting a conversation can be quite a task. The struggle can be evident which can make the person on the other end feel uncomfortable, not to mention the awkward feeling we get.

Once you master the art of small talk, you will never have to worry again. You don't have to dread a dinner party, a first date, or any other potentially awkward event that might put you on the spot, grasping for words to say, and wracking your brain to find something of value to talk about. Talk about nothing! It worked for Seinfeld and it will work for you too.

## What is Small Talk?

Small talk is like a snack. It is…just a little piece. It can serve a number of purposes. It might be all you have, just like when you are hiking and you need a protein bar for nourishment. You may have a snack to enjoy while relaxing. A snack can tide you over until a full meal; and it can be a teaser before the main course, similar to an appetizer.

Small talk is when you speak about non-controversial, seemingly unimportant, or trivial matters such as the weather or a sports game you watched on television. Basically, it's talking about nothing. Don't underestimate it, though. "Seinfeld" was a television show about nothing that ran nine straight seasons and was hailed by TV Guide as the World's Best Television Show EVER! Millions tuned in to watch it every week. I know. I was one of them. Almost two decades later, a significant number of people still watch the reruns. I do that too. I actually have many of them memorized. So why do I and so many other people love the show? Personally, I love the fact that I can just enjoy the characters talking about nothing. It requires no concentration, no analysis, no judgements to make or any other kind of thinking. I just get to listen to them talk.

"Hey, Joe! How's the weather?" You might ask your friend. "Fine," he might answer. "You know Texas in July. It's a scorcher but it's not been too bad."

Now, that's small talk. It's a leisure chat about nothing.

When you call your friend in Texas after a tornado and have a talk about the weather, that's quite the contrary. "Hey, Joe! How's the weather?" You might ask. "Oh man," he might reply. "A category 5 touched down right across the street from me. My neighbors are missing and our home is unlivable. We are homeless, Jim. Can we come stay with you for about six months while the insurance fights over our claim?"

Now THAT is…not small talk.

As mentioned before, small talk is a lot like a snack. It can be dished out for different purposes, just as a food snack is. It can tide you over to get to the meat of your conversation. It can serve as the main dish if that suits your purpose. You can small talk for pleasure and you can use small talk to whet your listener's appetite while waiting for the main dish.

## Here's How It Is Done

There are endless approaches to begin your small talk. Here are some of my favorite ways:

- **Ask a question.** What's even better is to ask a question about the person you are talking to or about something you know interest him.

- **Take a look around the room.** Something will spark an idea in you. Lay the subject out on the table, providing it isn't about your boss' wife flirting with the Personnel Manager or something inappropriate or controversial. If you see a smart phone and are talking to a tech geek, get his opinion on the latest model that is out.

- **Brainstorm.** This is done much like the above except, rather than going with what you see, it will be what you think. A bear comes to mind. The person next to you used to live in the mountains of Colorado. Ask if he or she has ever seen a bear there. It's great if you can ease into the small talk by maybe mentioning a bear. "I saw on the news that a camper was attacked by a bear last week. Did you ever encounter one when you lived in Colorado?"

- **In the event that the person you are wishing to talk to jumps the gun and asks you a question, feel free to answer with a question.** A good way to do so is: "So tell me about your vacation this summer…" You can turn it to focus back on him or her by, "Speaking of vacations, I hear you took a fabulous cruise…" Don't worry. People are rarely offended by getting to talk about themselves. In fact, you will soon learn that it's quite the contrary.

## Why will it get you off the hook?

Small talk will get you off the hook most every time. Why? Because you are shifting the focus. You are no longer on the spot to think of something of great importance to say but rather, you are casually talking…about nothing. Try it. It works for me and will work for you, too. Besides, it's fun once you get the hang of it.

## How to Make Small Talk Work for You

Sometimes talking is just…simply talking, but there are times that talking is really important. A job depends on it. A promotion is at hand…or at stake. When you are not one who can communicate easily and you are faced with a situation that greatly depends on what you say or don't say, it's time to pull your resources out. That is what I'm here to give you.

You can use small talk to do the following:

- **Allow yourself to catch your breath and slow down your heart rate**. Take deep breaths as you talk back and forth about the weather. Think of things like a waterfall or slow moving stream or…the person across from you sitting in his underpants.

- **Collect your thoughts.** You are about to have the most important job interview of your life and you can barely remember your name much less tell some important stranger about the duties you performed at a job ten years ago. As you strike up a small conversation about the game last night, take a few minutes to organize your thoughts.

- **Open up the person you are talking to.** Your new girlfriend's father is staring you down. He thinks you are a loser. In fact, he's sure of it. But wait. Did you mention vintage cars? He just happens to have one and perhaps he would love to show it to you. He has owned a few others too, and now, he wants to tell you all about them. He has totally forgotten about you. He is thinking about himself and his precious cars.

- **Find a common ground.** This is much like the scenario above but you are interested in the topic of small talk, too. You are meeting with a potential new client and your nerves are on edge. What can you say to win her over? The new account would mean a huge difference in your pocketbook, but you are at a loss. Is that a designer dress she's wearing? You just happen to love designer dresses and you have a fair share of knowledge about those, too. What a coincidence! So does she.

Talking may never be your passion. You may never volunteer to stand in front of hundreds of people to give a speech. But, it doesn't have to be your downfall either. No longer do you have to lose jobs, promotions, clients and potential relationships because of your "disability". You are now armed with a great tool called "small talk". It may be small and it may be about nothing but if you use it to your advantage, it is powerful and it will get the job done.

## Meet Joe and Mary

Mary and Joe are having a business meeting. They have worked together for years online. But, they have never met. Now, Joe has attended a motivational speaking event and he is pumped up to share what he has learned with Mary.

Mary on the other hand is nervous. She's a writer, not a talker. She worries because she didn't get a chance to get her hair color touched up. As she waits at Starbucks, she kept thinking about her roots rather than the meeting.

Joe appears and is all smiles. They introduce themselves to each other and Joe wastes no time in asking Mary about her day.

"It was fine," she tells him. Her heart is racing as she over-stirs her cappuccino. She wishes her husband had come along. He's so good at conversation. She knows Joe wants to hear about her day and get to know her but the words just don't come. Talking has never been her thing, especially to a boss she is just now meeting and…with roots.

She grapples for something to say. She is desperate. Then, she thinks back to a book she read years ago about such tense situations. Small talk. Surely she can talk about…nothing.

Joe has just come back from hearing a motivational message. She once wrote a motivational book. "What's your favorite motivational quote?" she asks.

Joe laughs. "Funny you should ask but I just heard it today. *Nothing changes unless something changes.*"

"You've got to be kidding," Mary giggles. "That's my all-time favorite too. I mean, how can it not be? That's how I quit smoking. I had to change everything. I always smoked in the car so I actually had to start walking everywhere. I'm serious…"

"I like that one about how bumblebees can't scientifically fly, that is. But they don't know it so…they fly. *If you think you can, you can. If you think you can't…well…you can't.* Something like that. You know."

Mary smiles. "I read his book when I was at a mountain cabin in Colorado. Quite insightful."

"Where in Colorado? I love Colorado."

"Telluride."

"Oh my goodness…I skied there some years ago."

"You ski? I love to ski…"

And so the small talk went. Several coffees and several hours later, the topic turned to business and was a successful meeting that led to a lot of great changes within the company and financial perks as well. The next meeting was in Telluride. They brought their families and had a wonderful ski trip. Not only had they become connected business wise but they became good friends as well.

You never know where small talk will take you.

## Some Social and Business Icebreakers to Get Your Juice Going

Here are some icebreaker activities that will help you get your feet wet so you can become a pro at starting small talk conversations.

The next time you are at a party, wedding or social gathering, do these three things.

- Go up to someone you don't know and start a conversation about the location you are at. It can be about the venue, the decorations, the amount of people at the gathering or anything else you chose to talk about in regards to the location.

- See who makes eye contact with you. Whoever it is, start a conversation with them about the weather.

- Initiate a small talk with someone you have never seen before and ask them for advice on the subject of your choice.

**Below are some examples of things you can say:**

- What do you think about the movie?

- What's your favorite thing to do on a rainy day?

- What's your favorite item of clothing?

- What type of food do you dislike?

- What is your favorite restaurant?

- What is your favorite T.V. show?

- What foods do you dislike?

- If you could go anywhere in the world on vacation, where would that be?

- What was your most memorable birthday?

- What is your favorite sport to watch?

- Most embarrassing moment you ever experienced?

- What is your hobby?

- What one thing would you really like to own? Why?

- What did you want to be when you were a child?

- What is your favorite flower?

- What was the last book you read?

- Do you like to dance?

- What is your favorite color?

- What's your favorite travel destination?

- Have you already been there or do you still want to go?

- What always makes you laugh?

- What's your idea of the perfect day?

- What is something about you that no one here knows about?

- How do you like your coffee/tea? ( sweet or salty)

- What is the most important quality you like in a friend?

- Describe your perfect day off.

- What is your all-time favorite movie?

These icebreakers are to be done at business events or anything involving the office or your place of work.

- Approach a fellow employee who you don't know and talk about something that is of non-significance. It does not have to be about work.

- When in a common area such as the breakroom, find someone you don't know and ask them a question.

- Go to someone with a higher position at work and ask their advice on a trivial matter.

**You can use some of these questions:**

- What do you enjoy the most about your profession?

- How did you come up with this idea?

- How did you get involved with this event?

- What's your favorite thing to do off the job?

- How did you get interested in this business/career?

- What are some of the challenges of your profession?

- What do you enjoy the most about your profession?

- What advice would you give somebody like me who is just starting out in your business?

- What has been your most important work experience?

- Do you have family in the area? What do they do?

- What's the latest news at work? (or in your industry?)

- What's the most difficult part of your job?

- What one thing would you do if you know you could not fail?

Congratulations! You have made a great stride towards learning the wonderful world of small talk. The more you do it, the more you'll get warmed up to it and the better at it you will become.

## Let's Meet the Six Honest Serving Men. (Who, What, When, Where, Why and How?)

In written communication, we are taught the five W's and one H. That is: who, what, when, where, why and how. These are the things that are of value when writing a story and telling one, too.

Knowing these six things will help you convey your message in a clear and precise way. They will help you organize your message and the way you present it as well.

Not only do the five W's and one H help you communicate what you are saying, they also make a difference in your communication itself. Who you are talking to, what you are saying to them, when you are saying it, where you are saying it at, why you are saying what you are saying and most importantly, how you are saying it will all add up to effective presentation…or not.

## Who

In his article "5 Secrets That Will Help You Master Conversation Skills", Time.com writer Eric Barker expressed that people tend to listen better to those whom they have something in common with. That is where "who" comes into play. Know who you are talking to, be it an individual, a small group or a large audience. Do your homework and find similarities to build upon. Find a way to relate to whoever it is you are going to be talking to. If you are speaking to a group of youth, learn the lingo and be as hip as you can be. If you are going for an interview, find a similar interest with your potential employer. Who you are talking to matters and when you take the time to find out more about them, the better your conversation will go.

## What

What you are talking about must matter or you wouldn't be talking about it at all. As previously mentioned, even if what you are saying isn't of monumental importance like "the house is on fire," it is important to you. Perhaps you are talking about the weather. It's raining. Does that mean your fishing trip is cancelled? Maybe you suffer from seasonal disorder and rain makes you gloomy and you are reaching out to a friend for support. Or, perhaps it is just a fact. It's raining. Knowing what you are saying will help others know what you are saying as well.

## When

Knowing when and when not to say something is imperative. Children learn this through trial and error, unfortunately. They often try to say something at an inopportune time, like a little girl asking if she can invite a friend for a sleep-over when Mom just walked in the door from to a tornado of a mess her younger sibling created while the babysitter was busy talking on the phone.

Adults are guilty of bad timing too. I have caught my own self complaining about trivial matters to a close friend whose spouse is ill with fourth-stage cancer. Two years ago I would have been in line to do so but the current timing has changed the situation.

Maybe you are trying to talk to someone where it is loud or there are other distractions. Waiting for a better time will most likely get you better results. Likewise, if the person or persons you are attempting to converse with are highly upset, overly excited, or are experiencing extreme emotions, it may also be best to find another time to talk. Being sensitive to the timing of your talk is vital.

## Where

Where you say what you say is important. Who is around is a huge factor to consider. If you are talking to a co-worker about your boss and other co-workers are around or heaven forbid, your boss is in listening range, all of these things most likely will determine how your conversation will be received. The persons you are talking to may be distracted by the fact that they will not want to get a bad reputation by being part of the conversation. They may be afraid of losing their job.

You may happen to be talking to someone at an inopportune setting. Trying to counsel a friend about his or her marriage problems while the two of you are in Walmart is less than ideal. On the other hand, if the two of you are at Starbucks, sitting at an obscure table with plenty of privacy, the timing might be perfect.

Knowing who you are talking to, what you are talking about, and being aware of your surroundings is wise.

## Why

Why are you saying what you are saying? Are you trying to get a job? Are you attempting to raise funds for a worthy cause? Maybe you are consoling someone, seeking consolation yourself, gossiping, or trying to get a subliminal message across. We all have motives to our conversations, good, bad, or indifferent. You may be concerned about a friend and talking to another friend about the issue at hand. Your intention may not be to gossip, but it may appear as if it is. By realizing that, you can be sure to clearly communicate what your motive is...and isn't. Be aware of why you are saying what you are saying and you are less likely to come across wrong and will be much more likely to come across effectively.

## How

Sometimes, what you DON'T say is even more important than what you do say. It is estimated that at least ninety-three percent of the message we convey comes across through non-verbal means. For instance, if you are telling your spouse how much you love and appreciate a gift you were just given but are frowning, he or she may not think you are sincere. If you are telling your boss you are sick and need the day off but are laughing and happy, he may have trouble believing you. In the same manner, standing before a group saying how honored you are to have the opportunity to share with them as you are yawning might not reinforce what you are saying very well. How you say something is often more important as what you are saying. When you complement what you are saying with HOW you are saying it, you will get the attention of your audience.

## Hot Topic of Conversation: What it All Boils Down To

In a recent article, VirtualSpeechCoach.com featured an article that broke the ninety-three percent non-verbal communication impression down even further. It estimated that fifty-five percent of the message relayed stems from body language and thirty-eight percent from the tone of your voice. With that in mind, we had better get busy addressing these key factors.

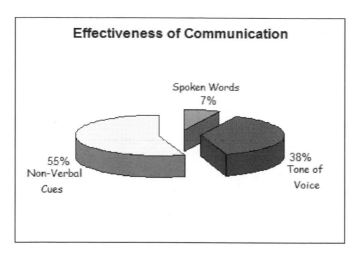

## Non-Verbal Communication Speaks Volumes

Non-verbal communication will either compliment or contradict what you are trying to impart when you talk. If you are talking to someone and have your arms folded to your chest, you most likely will give the appearance of being upset or close-minded. If you are talking to someone yet looking at something else, you will appear unfocused and distracted. As a result, that person will probably become unfocused and distracted as well. Learning about body language is very helpful when working to communicate effectively.

Body language is oftentimes done without thinking. That is how you can get in trouble with it or be misunderstood because of it. Being constantly conscious of your body language is vital to expressing yourself effectively. You can also get accustomed to reading other people's body language so you can implement your five W's and one H.

**Here are some implied basic body language meanings:**

- Crossing your arms can imply close mindedness, aggression, and/or general negativity.

- Wearing sunglasses can give the impression that you are hiding something.

- Sitting behind a desk creates a barrier and projects the feeling of superiority.

- A closer distance signifies you want to communicate on a more personal level.

- Getting too close gives the impression that you are invading personal space.

- A smile invokes positivity, happiness, and a general pleasant tone.

- Tilting your head on your elbow usually implies intense interest.

- Placing one or both hands in the pocket is a general indication one wants to get away from the conversation.

- Talking (or listening) with your head down gives the implication you are, or feel that you are, inferior.

**Here are some things to try on your own:**

- Be sure to stand at a good distance from the person or persons you are talking to. When talking to an individual, don't get too close but be sure that you are not too far away either. Learn to read the comfort zones of people you are talking to. When public speaking, of course, you will be further, but if the opportunity presents itself, coming out from behind the podium and walking down from the stage are good, personal gestures.

- Make eye contact. This isn't easy for some of us. Do it anyway. You don't have to stare. Just make it as casual and comfortable as you can. If it is really difficult for you to do, practice by doing it a little at a time until it becomes a comfortable practice.

- Pay attention to your body language. Be aware of the things you may be doing that may turn people off or cause unwanted effects on them.

- Make your body language work for you. Take the last suggestion a step further and implement some body language to reinforce and complement what you are saying. You can also add motions and gestures that go along with your conversation. Have fun with your talking and you'll be fun to listen to.

- Read the body language of the person you are talking to. If they are crossing their arms, you may need to be more persuasive. If they are yawning, get more enthused so they will follow as well.

## Toning Up Your Tone

"Don't look at me in that tone of voice," my mother used to say. What got me in even more trouble was TALKING in "that" tone of voice.

Your tone of voice sets the mood for what you are saying. It is HOW you say it that makes a lot of difference. Tone is the general feeling, quality, or attitude that is expressed when you are speaking.

Indeed, using the wrong tone of voice can get you into trouble. Trust me on that. My parents were not strict by any means, but when it came to the tone in which I spoke to them (and others) in, they were very stern. Why? Because the tone in which words are spoken with, exposes the heart.

If your boss gives you an assignment and tells you it is due tomorrow, chances are, you will say, "Alright." That is an affirmative word. You might just as easily reply with, "Ok". Any affirmative, agreeing word would be appropriate in this situation. But, your attitude comes forth in the tone you use in your response. If your tone is negative, annoyed, sarcastic, or defiant, you might as well have just said, "No!"

It is estimated that most arguments between couples have little to do with the words being spoken, but are 90% influenced by the tone of voice the words are spoken with. The same is true in general conversation. You will have a lot of trouble convincing someone of anything just by your words if the attitude behind your voice does not match up.

While tone can certainly be a downfall as it was for me in my teenage years where my parents were concerned, it can just as easily be a positive factor. With some knowledge and a little polishing, you can have your tone of voice reinforcing your every word. You can indeed influence your conversations and drive home your points. Toning up your tone will get your message across.

Some of the variations and connotations with tone of voice are:

- **Too loud** - intimidating, over-powering, tends to invite people to shut you out or become offensive.

- **Too soft** - makes you sound intimidated or like you are not the authority on the subject matter.

- **Sarcastic** - tends to anger those around you and project disrespect.

- **Monotone** - b-o-r-i-n-g!

- **Angry** - can make others angry to either at you or along with you. If anger is directed at the person you are speaking to, it is most likely that the person will become angry or shut you off.

- **Shaky -** uncomfortable to listen to, don't get the feeling they are sure of themselves or their subject matter. When someone is speaking in public and his voice is shaking with nervousness, the audience generally misses the message because they feel anxious and sorry for the nervous speaker.

- **Friendly -** tends to invoke a spirit of camaraderie and is generally a great way to get people's attention.

Here are some exercises for training your voice tone:

**Listen to others.** When someone is speaking, either in a presentation, a small group, or to you individually, listen to their tone. How does their tone affect you? By determining how other people's tone affects you, you will be aware of how your tone of voice may affect other people as well.

**Pay attention to how you are perceived.** As you speak to others, pay close attention to how your tone is being perceived. Are they yawning? Better pep it up a notch. Are they getting defensive? You should turn your tone down to a friendlier level.

**Listen to yourself.** Sometimes it's almost impossible to know how we really sound like without consciously hearing ourselves. Most people despise hearing themselves and there's a good reason why. We usually sound different than the way we think we do.. Record your voice and play it back. Critique your tone of voice and the message it is relaying to others. By finding the flaws, you can correct these.

**Listen to yourself from behind a microphone.** Hearing your voice on a tape recorder is one thing but if you speak behind a mic, you will hear the slightest details. From here, you can work on your tone even more intensely, especially if you are going to do any speaking activities that will entail the use of a microphone.

**Listen and watch yourself on video.** When you not only hear yourself but watch yourself on video, too, you will get a whole new view on how you converse. Watch your body language and listen to your tone as well. It can be a pain to watch at times but you will realize how differently you project yourself than you think you did.

I once took a class on interviewing. We had to be interviewed on video and then it was played back for the class to critique. I had a horrible hang-up with stage fright during those days. I felt like I was having a panic attack during the interview. But when it was played back to the class, the feedback I received was completely the opposite of what I thought it would be. "You appear to not care," the instructor summed up. "You seem so nonchalant and too underwhelmed with it all." On the contrary, it was a HUGE deal to me. I almost threw up during the taping. My stomach was so bundled up in nerves. That is not the picture I projected, though.

**Take a speech or acting class**. It will be fun, they said! Did I mention I used to have severe stage fright? Well, I did. That is why I enrolled in an acting class. We had to write our own skits and I aced that. In fact, I got a really great job offer out of the deal. But when it came to speaking before others, I was the worst in the class. But, once I let go and allowed myself to have fun and enjoy the class, the people and the shows we put on, I improved by leaps and bounds.

**Voice lessons.** That's right…voice lessons. If you can afford to take professional ones, do it. Singing lessons qualify as voice lessons. But, if you don't have the money to spend on lessons, you can try doing it on your own. Here's how:

- Practice raising your voice, lowering it, and hitting notes in between.

- Use various pitches in combination with different volumes.

- Practice body movement along with the lessons above.

- During practice, incorporate the emphasis of certain keywords or phrases.

  - Saying a word louder puts focus on it such as the word "hate" in the sentence, "I HATE bananas."
  - Try saying a sentence and slow it down, lowering your voice when you get to a certain word.
  - Pausing after the keyword encourages you to listen and to focus on it.

Practice makes perfect, so doing it over and over again is the name of the game. Once you feel you are up for it, find an audience and see how well you do. If you didn't quite hit the mark, practice some more and then try again.

*"It is not what you say that matters but the manner in which you say it; there lies the secret of the ages."*

\- William Carlos Williams

# Chapter Takeaways

1. Communication is the key to almost everything in life. It's THAT important.

2. By listening to yourself and others, you will improve your communication skills.

3. Tone is very important in conversation.

4. Body language plays a great role in communication.

# Chapter 4

# Communication Breakdowns:
# What is Holding You Back ?

*"Communication works for those who work at it."*

- John Powell

## What is Communication Breakdown?

Communication breakdown is when an interruption happens during the exchange or expression of information, ideas, thoughts or feelings. The breakdown may occur for a number of reasons and the results may vary, but they are never good. Communication is a vital part of human interaction; therefore, when it is broken, problems abound.

According to an article in the Huffington Post, communication breakdown is the number one reason behind divorces. In the article, a study by YourTango.com concluded that 65% of all divorces are caused by the inability to communicate. That's a lot of divorces!

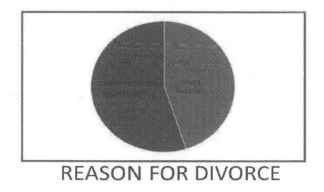

REASON FOR DIVORCE

Communication breakdown is not only a marital issue. It is a problem in every arena of life. If you cannot communicate effectively in the workplace, you are going to end up having problems with your employer, employees, clients or customers, and everyone else you deal with. Communication is vital in the workplace just as it is vital in a marriage.

Communication is necessary for practically anything we do and it needs to take place in most everywhere we go. It is imperative to express and exchange information, thoughts, feelings, or ideas in order to have a happy and productive life.

When it comes to communication, it is also important to know that there are people whose careers revolve around fixing communication breakdowns. There are marriage counselors, court mediators, and communication coaches that do nothing but help repair communication breakdowns.

What is at the root of communication breakdown? There are a good number and combination of factors that can cause communication malfunction. Of course, the problem may come from the one talking, the one listening, or both.

As we take a look at some of the most common core problems, you may note that you have one, some, or all. But…don't panic. Once you have identified the problem or problems, you can fix it. And don't worry about that part. That's exactly why you are reading this book. Remember, I taught myself to effectively communicate with anyone and…I'll teach you too!

## Physical Conditions

There are physical conditions that can hinder communication. If you have had a stroke, you may experience some limitations with your speech. If you stutter, you will also have some added issues when it comes to communication. Although physical conditions can get in the way of communicating, they don't have to prevent it. You will have to go the extra mile if you have a handicap that causes complications in communication. By taking advantage of the therapies and treatments available and by incorporating the information in this book, you will be well on your way to communicating to the best of your ability, which is exactly what we are all striving to do.

Mild to moderate physical disorders include stuttering, articulation issues, and problems processing what is being said. According to publication on communication disorders on Psychology Today's website, one out of every ten Americans live with or at least have at one time experienced a problem with speech. Mental retardation, drug abuse, and developmental disorders are among the top reasons for such issues. There is help available, though. Professional and self-help are abundant. If you suspect that your communication problem has roots in one of those areas, know that you can seek help at a further level as well as by gleaning from this book.

## Mental and Emotional Conditions

Some mental conditions cause impaired communication. Of those, some are severe such as mental retardation, while others have conditions that are less debilitating, but still hinder communication.

One condition is ADHD. It's difficult to hold a conversation on the talking or the listening end when you can't concentrate or keep your focus. There are exercises you can do to correct this. You can build your focus level up by doing some heavy concentrating on one thing for five minutes without interruption. Then, increase it to ten minutes, then, fifteen, and so forth. You may not reach the ultimate level, but you will certainly improve.

Depression is a very common condition these days. Life is complicated and overwhelming. Sometimes, we just aren't quick to rise above it. We fall into depression. Some experience depression chronically. It is more difficult to communicate when you are depressed, but it is a very helpful thing to do if you are experiencing depression. It is like trying to put one foot in front of the other and walk your way through this book out of commitment rather than base on how you feel about it. The information in this book will help you talk to others about your feelings and it will enable you to communicate with others in a better way. It will also help you when talking to a counselor or in group setting counseling sessions.

## Panic Attacks

A panic attack falls into the physical, mental, and emotional categories. It is all of the above. If you have ever gone in to talk to your boss about a raise and found yourself shaking like a leaf, sweating up a storm, and barely able to breathe, you have experienced a panic attack to some degree. I used to get them without fail when speaking before a group. Even in a small group setting, I would find my voice shaking beyond control. I could barely focus because I was so dizzy. My heart beats out of my chest. It wasn't fun. It was humiliating. I had to find a cure.

There are a number of exercises you can do in order to help prevent or control a panic attack that interferes with your communication.

Here are some suggestions:

- Picture your audience, be it one person or many, in their underwear. It's true. By thinking of your audience in an awkward situation rather than focusing on your own discomfort, you are likely to overcome.

- Breathe deep and regularly. Many people tend to hold their breath or breathe too hard and too fast when nervous. By steadying your heart, you steady your entire mind and body which makes it easier to communicate.

- Think of the peacock and the stork. A counselor once told me that when I panic when speaking it is a very selfish thing. I am concerned with how I look, how I sound, how "I this and how I that". If I were to focus on the message, I am wanting others to hear as well as on them, I divert the self-centeredness. "Pride is a peacock all proud. Pride is also a stork burying his head in the sand," he told me. Pride is self-centered, whether saying, "Look at me or don't look at me." That hit home to me and was one of the major plays in my winning game to overcome my fear of speaking.

- Whatever calms you, implement it. If music soothes you, listen to your favorite tunes just before talking. If you are one that likes to write, write. If you are an essential oil fan, use lavender or an oil that relaxes your mind. Whatever it is that sends you to a better state of mind, use it to or do it.

## Soul Searching

Diagnosing the problem is where it all begins. A doctor does a check-up to see what the ailment is. He may order further tests. A good doctor doesn't stop until he has found the issue. A mechanic diagnoses your car before working on it to see where the problems lie. Finding the problem is the first step in finding the answer.

In this chapter, we have looked at some of the causes behind communication breakdowns. You may have one, all, or none of these. You may have one that wasn't touched on. You may not be sure which, if any, you have.

It is important to do some soul searching so you can diagnose your communication problem or problems. If you are unsure, you might ask a trusted friend or a counselor. You can also start paying closer attention to what you are thinking and feeling and what is going on around you when the breakdown occurs.

For example, maybe you and your spouse get along great...most of the time. But there are times when you argue and you cannot communicate your feelings. It starts to take a toll on your marriage. You long to diagnose the problem so you can fix it. You can ask your spouse for feedback which may or may not be constructive. Seek the advice of a counselor to make an accession. Alternatively, you can also go over the details of what takes place when the breakdown occurs. Is it when you are drinking alcohol? Do the spats tend to happen when one or both of you are overstressed or really tired? Maybe you are carrying around emotional baggage from childhood or from a previous failed relationship. Diagnosing the problem will help prepare you for the next chapter--solutions to problems. Let's not waste another minute! Let's get fixed!

## Chapter Takeaways

1. There's nothing to be ashamed of in having a communication problem. What is shameful is not identifying it and not fixing it.

2. Some communication problems are physical, such as speech impediments.

3. Some issues with communication are emotional, such as low self-esteem.

4. All problems can be worked on. You can master your fate when you diagnose the problems, because then you can find the solution and I am here to help.

# Chapter 5

# Now We're Talking

*"The way we communicate with others and with ourselves ultimately determines the quality of our lives."*

- Tony Robbins

## The Solution

The sole reason for diagnosing the problems with communication in the preceding chapter was to do one thing--to fix what's broken. Get ready to mend it.

In the next chapter, we are going to stretch and build our communication skills by way of some unique and awesome exercises. We will work on removing barriers and solving problems by doing some constructive drills. But before we proceed, it's important to get warmed up, like what an athlete does before a competition.

## Pumping Up

It is important to get pumped up physically and mentally. A football player pumps iron to build muscles. Cheerleaders cheer them to victory. Coaches offer pep talks. It's all in the game...you've got to pump it up.

One of the main root problems behind poor communication is the lack of confidence. While you may have read the last chapter and diagnosed a multitude of underlying conditions for your poor communication skills, chances are good that behind those factors lies a pesky problem called low self-esteem. Let's take a look at what that really means.

Nine times out of ten, when you have a low esteem of yourself, it stems from comparing yourself to others. Sixty year olds who compare their bodies to eighteen year-olds are most likely going to come up on the raw end. Girls who compare their looks to super models eventually find out that it is not a wise idea to do so. On the same note, if you are measuring your communication skills against a motivational speaker or an actor or actress right at the beginning, you may not come out so well. You should council from the great but always focus on improving your skills one step at the time.

Self-confidence shows in the way you speak. You either have it or you don't; and it shows. People flock to those who are steadfast, while they tend to shy away from those who are weak. If you don't have it, then get it. Yes, it's that easy. You hold the key. You are in charge if you chose to be. Here are some great things you can do to boost your self-confidence:

- Make a conscious decision RIGHT NOW to become self-confident.

- Change what you don't like about yourself. If you think you are rude, work at being a nicer, more considerate person. If you don't like your looks, do what you can to improve them and also determine to focus on inner-beauty as well.

- Make a daily list of ten things you like about yourself. Grab a pen and paper and start RIGHT NOW!

- Ask a trusted friend 10 things they like about you.

- Every day, recall 10 things you have done successfully.

- Praise yourself for every step you take forward.

- Treat yourself to rewards like a special coffee, a good read or a long soak in the tub.

- Verbally tell yourself in the mirror that you are a good and worthy person.

- Forgive yourself for shortcomings.

- Know that you are as good as everyone else

OK, so, if you truly do the steps above, you are well on your way in becoming more confident. You will begin to see yourself in a whole new light and others will see you the same way. You will learn to respect yourself more and others will follow suite. As the famous psychiatrist and television talk show host, Dr. Phil McGraw says, "You teach people how to treat you." It's true. You are in the driver's seat.

## Input, Output

If you want a positive output (speech), you must have a positive input. It is vital to read good material, talk to great people, and to surround yourself with ideas and personalities you want to be like. If you hang out with a negative crowd, you are going to wreak of negativity. If you spend your time with positive people, you will reflect such. Chose books that motivate you. Listen to music that brings out the best in you and think about good things.. You will project positivity in your communication and that attracts the results that you are longing for. People will flock to hear what you have to say when you are soaking in the good and pouring it out in return.

## Put it Into Action

So you've done your pumping and watched your intake to assure you only input positive things, now it's time to put it all into action. Here are some exercises that will project the confidence you are acquiring as you continue the lessons:

1.  Stand with a confident posture and hold your head high.

2.  Make eye contact!

3.  Remember to smile and you will be rewarded when you see, firsthand, how contagious your smile is.

4.  Laugh and see how others respond.

5.  Own the conversation. You are THAT good.

6.  Be prepared for random conversations by keeping up with current events and studying off-the-wall interesting topics.

7.  Believe in yourself and soon others will, too.

8.  Have fun watching the new way your communication skills are touching others. It's a win-win situation, for sure!

# Chapter Takeaways

1. Once you have diagnosed the problems within your communication skills, you can fix them. I'll show you how!

2. If you have conditions that require a doctor or counselor, don't hesitate to employ that you're your lesson plan. You are worth it!

3. Pump yourself up, mentally and physically. The effort you put it equals the results you will bring out.

4. Positive input equals positive output. - Zig Ziglar

5. Putting what you learn into action is the key. Many people miss great communication skills because they don't apply what they have learned. Knowing is not enough you must do.

# Chapter 6

# Brain Talk: Communication is a Brain Thing

*"Communication is all in the mind."*

-Author Unknown

## How it Works: Taking Sides

Everything we do starts out in the brain in one way or another. The brain is an amazing thing.

The brain is separated into two hemispheres: the left side and the right side. No doubt you've heard this all your life. Those who are said to be left-brained are the more logical thinkers; while artists, writers, and all-around dreamers have been deemed right-brained. While this concept continues to be challenged, the fact is that most,(not all) have their language skills housed in their left brain.

For years, it has been said that speech comes from the left side of the brain, but recent studies show that this may not be entirely true. There are many aspects of speech and even more where true communication is concerned. It is being discovered that a number of brain territories are used.

When you think of what you are going to say and how you are going to say it, the process involves the left frontal lobe of your brain which is just behind your eyebrow. This area is known for creativity which is exactly what this type of processing calls for.

You are going to tell of an event which is much like recreating the story; so, you must call upon your descriptive words and appropriate phrases. The same is true for coming up with a speech to give. Before you utter a word, your left frontal lobe is in action...or maybe not. For those who have trouble communicating properly or have problems coming across in an interesting manner, this process is oftentimes weak. It seems that some of us who are writers have more trouble than others communicating via orally than by pen and paper or keyboard as is the case these days.

The right side of the brain plays an important part in speech as well. It is less on the objective part and more apt to interpret things like jokes, abstract phrases, play-on words, and such. It is the part that can decipher connotations and underlying messages. The right side "gets it" where the left is more sensible and descriptive.

The pre-motor side of your brain organizes what you are about to say such as grammar and the method for relaying your message. The motor side actually says the words and generates the words. It is in the left hemisphere of your brain.

## Going Head to Head

Communication is a two-way set up. The science behind it can get complicated. It depends on the speech and listening functions of two people. That complication got plenty of people fired, cost many couples their marriages, and has been the root of many teenage rebellions. Just one little glitch and communication can be botched, causing heartache, hatred, and a myriad of other issues. This is the reason why it is so important to master communication skills. Your quality of life depends upon it.

While you cannot control the actions and reactions of others, you can influence them. And, you can do so in a way that works to your favor. You can implement all the lessons taught in this book so that you can convey your ideas, feelings, and information in a well-packaged and positive manner taking into consideration all you have learned about body language, tone of voice, timing of your talk, subject material, self-confidence projecting behind your conversation, smiles (of course), and the implementation of your listening skills as well.

With those things working for you, you will stand the best chance of having a productive two-way communication. You will be doing your best and at the same time, be influencing your listener, too. You will be making it easier for the other person or persons to follow through with their side of the conversation.

For instance, if you are talking to someone in a monotone voice about a very boring subject in the middle of the Super Bowl game with a frown on your face, you are probably not going to get a very good response. But, if you implement what you know about timing of your talk with a beautiful smile on your face while sounding excited about the subject, which the recipient also finds interesting, you are improving the odds that you'll have a great conversation between you and the listener.

## Speak Your Mind: Brain Games for Improving Communication

Communication is a cognitive skill that allows you to meaningfully interact with others. Scientists have proven that brain games improve your ability to communicate. But, the catch is, the games must be performed regularly in order to truly make a long-lasting and permanent difference.

Here are some great ways to improve your communication skills within your brain:

- Play word games with others or with yourself as often as possible.
  Games include: Scrabble, Scattergories, BananaGram, and the like.

- Brainstorming helps you learn to quickly unscramble random thoughts in your brain and use them in a conversation. Look up and the first thing you see is your topic of conversation. Talk to yourself for five minutes about the topic. Implement those things you have learned so far to help make your conversation worth listening to.

- Watch any television show for thirty minutes. See what you can gather from each character's style of communication and note what you do and do not like about each style. How can you put what you have learned into your own communication skills or lack thereof?

- List five things you would like to improve about your conversations. List five things you can do about the previous five. Do them!

- Think about what you thought about before, during, and after you talk. Work on controlling each of these stages.

## Mind Matters: It Doesn't Take a Rocket Scientist

Although the subject of communication is certainly one that is a neuroscience favorite, it doesn't take a rocket scientist to know that there is something within the brain that makes people want to talk about themselves. It comes across as somewhat egocentric and, in a way, it has to be classified as such because it is built around oneself. But, when you think about it, it's only natural. We are surrounded by ourselves every minute of every day, of course, we want to talk about what is familiar to us.

In the article, "The Neuroscience of Everybody's Favorite Topic" by Adrian Ward which was published on the Scientific American website, the question is raised, why do people like to spend so much time talking about themselves? It is estimated that people spend 60 percent of their conversation on themselves. But, why?

Studies have been conducted on subjects who were given the assignment to talk about themselves. The results revealed that three neural regions in particular were stimulated by this activity: the prefrontal cortex, the nucleus accumbens, and the ventral tegmental area. The latter two came as a surprise. They have much to do with dopamine, the "feel good" substance within the brain that is often associated with things like cocaine, sex, and great food. Amazingly, these areas were stimulated even if there was no one listening to the subjects. As it turns out, just talking about oneself causes the effect, regardless if there is an audience or no interaction at all. Interesting!

It was concluded that perhaps the reason the brain reacts in such a way is for survival. For this reason, people are encouraged by their own brain to communicate about themselves. When you think about it, talking about yourself can be therapeutic. It can also express your needs, both physical and emotional. It is a means to gain companionship. There are many things that talking about yourself ultimately accomplishes which are not all just ego-based and for prideful reasons.

The results of this study show that it is very natural and quite acceptable to a certain extent to talk about yourself. In application, try this. If you are looking for a subject to strike up a good, long-lasting conversation with someone, try to bring out a topic about that person. Ask them questions about themselves. Find out what interests them and chose your topic accordingly. Give them something to talk about--themselves. You can't go wrong!

## Chapter Takeaways

1. Speech and communication are functions of the brain. Certain parts of the brain control various aspects involved in communicating with others.

2. When you take part in creating a conversation or deciphering the punch line of a joke, the frontal left brain is used. Amazing!

3. You can do word games, such as Scrabble, in order to stimulate your brain for a more effective communication.

4. Some aspects of communication are done on the right part of your brain and some are on the left.

5. It is a scientifically proven fact that people like to talk about themselves. Knowing this can help win you a person's attention during a conversation.

# Chapter 7

# Personality Plus: The True Secrets of Communication

*"The single biggest problem in communication is the illusion that it has taken place."*

\- George Bernard Shaw

## The Extra Mile

There are a number of methods you can use to learn to efficiently and effectively communicate with others. You can do all the exercises from A to Z. You can learn to pitch your voice perfectly, say what you mean and mean what you say, move your body in the right way, but there will always be something missing.

Some things just attract us to listen to a person and other things do quite the contrary. Do you like talking to someone who is drab and self-centered? How do you feel about speaking to someone who doesn't appear to be paying the slightest bit of attention to you? On the other hand, how do you feel after someone talks to you who is smiling ear-to-ear, genuinely happy to hear your every word and have a great, two-way conversation? There's a world of difference.

In going the extra mile, you will be able to talk to anyone, anywhere, and get the results you are looking for. You won't just be talking to walls and likewise, talking to you won't be like talking to a wall. Real communication is always worth going to the extra trouble to make your efforts complete. It's like icing on the cake. Let's get to baking!

## I Want What He's Got: The Art of Smiling

You've probably heard of the notorious book written in 1936 by the self-improvement guru, Dale Carnegie, entitled *"How to Win Friends and Influence People"*. You may have even read the book or at least have heard witty quips of it like "Your smile is a messenger of your good will. Your smile brightens the lives of all who see it. To someone who has seen a dozen people frown, scowl or turn their faces away, your smile is like the sun breaking through the clouds."

While Mr. Carnegie's words are true indeed, on the flip side, a smile doesn't necessarily win approval and a listening ear. As author Leil Lowndes points out in his book, "How to Talk to Anyone- 92 Little Tricks for Big Success in Relationships", a smile can certainly be the key to communication or it can lock you out of it.

We've all experienced that smiling salesman that has a fake grin plastered on. He has a smile because he's supposed to have one. He has one thing in mind. He wants to make money off you. That kind of smile is a sure turn-off.

On the other hand, there are those with a smile as contagious as a yawn. They smile at you and you automatically smile back. These people brighten up your day and make you want to listen to them. You want to hear what they have to say. You want what they've got.

So what it adds up to is that yes, Mr. Carnegie is absolutely correct. So is Leil Lowndes. A smile can, for sure, make you a superstar talker but only if it is the right kind. The wrong smile, like a fake grin or a sarcastic one, can win you a deaf ear from the get-go. It's important that your smile be just right so that it can work for you and not against you. In fact, it's so important I am devoting a good bit of information on the subject. Ready?

**The importance of a smile.** A smile is like a ray of sunshine. It's one of the first ways babies learn to communicate and we as parents get so excited. While babies cry from day one, when they smile, it's a milestone. They are communicating more than just their wants and needs, they are communicating feelings. A baby is happy so a baby smiles. There's nothing sweeter. Not only do we smile when we are happy, seeing others smile tends to make us happy as well.

**The science of a smile.** In an article on Forbes.com, *"Untapped Power of Smiling"*, Ron Gutman explains the science behind a smile.

In his article, Gutman summed it up like this: *"Smiling stimulates our brain's reward mechanisms in a way that even chocolate, a well-retarded pleasure inducer, cannot match."*

So what is it that is so spectacular that transpires within the brain when we smile that could possibly make it better than almighty chocolate? Here's the deal: A positive thing takes place. A neuronal signal goes from your brain's cortex to the old brain (brainstem) and then the signal travels to the cranial muscles where a message goes to the smile muscles in your face and…bingo…a smile appears. But wait a minute, there's more! Then there's a loop of positive feedback that goes from your smile to your brain and a sensation of joy occurs. Wow! That's something to smile about!

**Smile and Dial.** I'm not exactly bragging on this, but I once was a telemarketer. Yes, I'm the one you hung up on. Or…maybe I'm one of the few telemarketers you actually took the time to talk to. Why? My boss had a mirror placed at each of our stations. It was  part of our job to smile. We were to smile in the mirror and to smile all the way through each and every call. You may be wondering what purpose that served when the person on the other end couldn't even see me? Surprisingly, smiling while talking can actually be heard. Try it. You'll see for yourself. I certain can attest to the fact. I got totally different reactions when I smiled as opposed to when I didn't and you will too no matter if the person or persons you are talking to can see you…or not.

**Fake it till you make it?** I'm sure you've heard the old adage, "Fake it till you make it." But does that go for a smile? While in some instances it does, think back to the salesman. A fake smile can indicate trickery, mockery and other negative connotations so proceed with caution. If you are trying to force a smile for the right reasons, trying to create happiness in yourself and others, then it's a total different story. We'll take a look at types of smiles and you'll get a better understanding of the difference in smiles.

**Power play.** Smiling is powerful. It is the perfect way to communicate your happiness and influence the happiness of others as well. When incorporated into verbal communication, there is nothing more powerful to get you heard. People will listen. They'll want what you have.

## Smiling Exercises

This is probably one of the most fun group of exercises you will ever be assigned. If you want to learn to make your smile genuinely work to better your communication skills, here are some lessons to love.

**Observe**. This is a really easy exercise and one that you might think is elementary, but I guarantee it is one of the most important and effective communication lessons ever. Start watching people's smiles or…their lack of. Which smiles are you attracted to? Which repulses you or sends a warning signal to your brain? Which one makes you want to smile back? Pay even closer attention when someone is talking and smiling. What reaction does their smile invoke?

**Types of Smiles.** As you observe different smiles, try to associate them with a feeling. There are happy smiles, smiles of pure joy, hesitant smiles, sarcastic smiles, half smiles and even sad smiles. Various smiles send different signals to the brain. THAT is why just faking a smile isn't always the most constructive thing to do. Here are examples of some smiles and their general connotation:

- Smug smile: arrogance

- Tight-lipped smile: fake

- Half smile: superiority or, in some instances, shyness

- Full open mouth smile: fake

- No eye-contact smile: deceit or deep thought

- Genuine smile: happy

**Imitate**. Humans learn by imitating. We've done that since we were born so, now is not the time to stop. When you see a great smile that brings about a great response in communication, mimic it. Don't worry. You're not stealing it. It is now your own and you too can pass it on. Incorporate the smile into your own conversations and see what kind of results you get. I think the outcome is going to make you…smile.

### Facts About Smiles:

- A single smile requires up to 53 facial muscles.

- Smiles are free.

- Smiles are contagious.

- Smiling can boost your mood.

- Smiling can strengthen your immune system.

- Smiling is a universal language.

- Smiles can reduce stress.

## Charisma

Charisma--we all know who's got it. It's that special someone who walks into a room and just lights it up. Their presence is always noted. The individuals that everyone gets attracted to are charismatic. You want to be with them. You want to be like them. Now, you can be.

Charisma is charm, a compelling attractiveness. It's not just a description of someone, it is an action word. It draws you in. It's a magnet.

For some really sweet icing on the cake when it comes to the art of conversation, charisma is what will never fail you. You will own the room, master the conversation and get the job. It's a combination of true happiness and confidence and a giving of that through yourself to others.

Either you have it or you don't? Not true. You can acquire charisma. The more you work on your inner self, the more your light will shine by way of charisma. Here are some things to work on that will make you a more charismatic person.

- Hang out with those who possess charisma. It's contagious. Let it rub off on you.

- Get excited! Be passionate! These things resonate from within and shine forth.

- Be confident. Charismatic people aren't prideful, they just know they are right. Why? Because the things they believe are true. They are all about things that cannot fail like the Golden

Rule and giving is better than receiving. They know the values they have are just and they carry themselves accordingly.

- Be genuinely interested in others. Take an interest in those who are around you or your charisma will turn to egocentric behavior and you'll come off as arrogant instead. Listen to others. Devote undistracted attention and interest in those around you.

- Listen and read about motivational inspiring things. What you take in is what will shine out.

- Be a leader! By taking charge to guide others, you will be able to share what you've got and that is what charisma is all about.

## Listen Carefully

Another action that will greatly enhance your people skills and your ability to communicate effectively is the art of listening. Trust me, it IS an art. It takes work and focus to listen to others because let's face it, sometimes we just aren't that interested in what they are saying. But, when you listen, you learn. Furthermore, your talking becomes a conversation, two or more people talking back and forth. And when two people are talking AND listening to one another…there is a magical thing called communication.

## Obstacles to Listening

When I taught myself to communicate with others, one of the first things I had to work on was my listening skills. I was a horrible listener and it was obvious. Not only was I often listening only to find something to say in return (self-centered listening), I am a multi-tasker so I was rarely listening with full attention. Furthermore, I was absorbed in my own thoughts much of the time. Instead of really hearing what the person who was talking to me was saying, I was oftentimes casting them as a character in my next book or daydreaming about something the conversation caused me to recall.

Whatever the specifics, I was being very rude. I was not being heard because...I was not listening. People pick up on that sort of thing and no one wants to talk to the wall or...listen to the wall they just talked to. Listening is a two-way street. If you want to gain the respect of being heard, you must give the respect of hearing in return.

Here are some common reasons people do not listen:

- Self-centeredness

- Actual hearing disability

- Distraction

- Disinterest

- Poor timing

- Pre-judging the subject

Examples of barriers in communication:

- Linguistics

- Physical

- Gender

- Religious

- Political

- Social Status

- Appearance

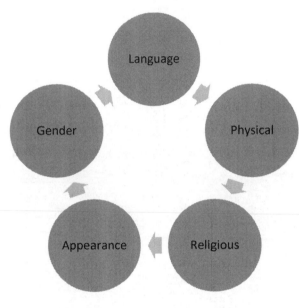

BARRIERS TO COMMUNICATION

## Listening Exercise

**Repeat.** When someone is talking to you, listen as though your life depended on it. If you were to need to tell the police every single word the person spoke to you for a life or death situation at hand, how much of the conversation would you recall? After hearing what was said, recall as much of it as possible with as many details as you can.

**Listen to hear, not to reply.** It's very common to listen with the intent to interject your own response into the conversation. It is natural, but not optimal. Rather than hearing to figure what you can say or how it affects you, try to listen and think of the person talking to you and how what he or she has to say affects him or her. Doing this will open your ears to a whole new line of thinking.

**Drawing conclusions, literally.** After someone has talked to you, the next available opportunity you have, draw a picture of what he or she said. It may just be a scribbling on the back of a sales receipt when you get to your car or it can be an oil painting masterpiece. It doesn't matter as long as you picture the impression that was imprinted on your from what they had to say. If it's just a blob, chances are you need to go back to the first exercise and work your way down again.

## Saying What They Want to Hear

People love to talk about what matters to them. In the article "The Art of Conversation: 5 Do's and 5 Don'ts" by Brett and Kate McKay on the TheArtof Manliness.com website, the fact is driven home. People not only like to talk about what matters to them and attract to people of similar interests, they also love to hear about themselves. They like to talk about themselves. Talking about the person you are talking to or at least take interest in topics that are dear to them is a guarantee to get you heard.

Here are some other points to ponder when it comes to great communication that the article offers:

- Find out the interests of the person or people you will be speaking to for your topic of conversation.

- Arm yourself with knowledge in regards to the subjects they are interested in.

- Be a great listening.

- Never interrupt.

- Tailor your conversation to the listener.

- Wait for your turn to speak.

- Think…think…think…before you speak.

## In Hindsight

So now you are making milestones in your journey to become a fantastic talker. You are well-equipped not only to speak and be heard, but to hear others as well which earns you conversations rather than lectures or speeches that are one-way streets. Congratulations, but don't stop here. There's more good stuff just around the bend.

*"Most people do not listen with the intent to understand; they listen with the intent to reply."*

\- Stephen R. Covey

Be different!!!

# Chapter Takeaways

1. Go the extra mile! When you take the time and make the effort to add the special effects to your communication skills, it will show.

2. Smile! Your smile will actually stimulate the brain of those around you to "feel good." That is pretty powerful!

3. When you work on your inward self, your light will shine by way of charisma. People will want to be around you and will want to hear what you have to say.

4. Listen to others. This unselfish act will help ensure your communication is a two-way street.

# Chapter 8

# Ten Communication Exercises That Really Work

*"Communication works for those who work at it."*

- John Powell

## Speak-Easy Exercises

Now that you have some really great background information and a few exercises under your belt, it's time to really stretch yourself. You have already done some of these communication drills so we'll just be combining those you already know with some new concepts as well. The more you get out of your comfort zone, the more you will grow. Remember, nothing changes unless you change it. Take control. Work on your program and learn to communicate effectively and efficiently to get what you want out of life. After all, it's the only one you'll get!

Confidence matters! Know that you can do this. You took the initiative to read this book and now, you are making it work for you. You are doing exactly what you need to do. You CAN do this thing!

Oh, and one more thing. It's great to keep a journal. Start today by writing down all the obstacles you have that are keeping you from your goal--effectively communicating.

## Top Ten Talk it Out Exercises

**Day One -** It's a brand new day! Wake up, wake up! That's right. Today can be a wake-up call for you as you begin your new life. Take it from me, being able to communicate is a whole new life. You'll see. Here is your homework for today:

- Begin the day with a positive motivational audio, book, or quote. Think about it all through the day.

- Listen and watch people talk all day. At the end of the day, decided which conversation was the best and which was the worst…and why.

**Day Two** - Remember the observation drill from yesterday? Now it's time to apply it to your personal communication skill lessons.

- Recall your favorite talker from yesterday. Remember what it was that he or she did that made their communication effective, interesting, informative, or whatever it was you liked about their way of talking. Imitate it in as many of your own conversations as possible. At the end of the day, access how you think you did. Continue to do these first two drills from now on, coming up with new people to model after as well.

**Day Three -** What are some skills your communication is lacking?

- Think of the areas your skills need the most work in and work on them today. If you tend to have poor judgement on timing your conversations, change that bad habit. If you don't even know what you are saying, work on not rambling and having a purpose in your talking. This isn't a one-day drill. This will be done from here on out. Change up what skills you work on so that you can perfect your skills one at a time.

**Day Four -** Smile because this is your day to shine.

- With each and every conversation you have today, smile. Once you see how much better the response you get is, you will always want to go the extra mile with a smile.

**Day Five -** Tone it up!

- Fine tune your communication by accessing your tone of voice. Listen to yourself. Ask a friend. Do whatever you need to do to diagnose what your tone needs in order to rock a conversation. Are you monotone? Add some pitch. Take into consideration the volume as well. Talking too loud or too soft is a problem. Solve it once you diagnose it. Let this be the day you change your tone forever. You will love the results.

**Day Six -** Eye contact is vital. People think you aren't really "there" for them if you don't look them in the eyes.

- While still incorporating the things above, commit to making eye contact with each person you talk to or who talks to you…from now on.

**Day Seven -** Put some icing on the cake! Whet their appetite to learn more about what you have to say by adding the frills.

- Make hand motions. Use facial and body motions. Give body signals that are positive.

**Day Eight -** Listen up! This is one of the most important drills ever and it is one that you will hold yourself accountable from now on.

- Listen to those around you. When you are talking, listen as well. When you are being spoken to, listen. Wait for the person you are communicating with to reply whether it is verbally or through a nod or some other body language. Listen and you'll get heard.

**Day Nine -** Remember people like to talk about themselves.

- Start conversations that will trend to the person you are talking to. Cater to their likes and dislikes and ask them questions that spur them to talk about their favorite subject-- themselves. See if you don't get astounding results by doing so.

**Day Ten -** Change your focus; change your life. Being able to communicate is life-changing. People skills are among the best skills to have and that is what communication boils down to--relating to people and people relating to you. By paying closer attention to what you say, how you say it, what others say, how they say it, and how others are perceiving what you say, this will open your eyes.

- Push yourself. Focus on everything that involves communication today. Adjust what needs to be adjusted. Change anything that needs to be changed. Improve what can stand improvement. Taking into account the above and all that you have learned in this book, get out of your comfort zone. Be the one who raises your hand in class. Step up to the mic at a sales meeting. Jump in the conversation you used to be intimidated of. The more you just get out there, the more you'll move up in life.

Congratulations! You have a great start to new communication skills. As long as you continue to repeat the drills and to advance forward in your self-accessing and stretching, you will continue to get better and better at communicating; and the better you get, the better results you will receive as well.

It's time to pull your journal back out. As you conquer your obstacles and road blocks, mark them off your list. Now, add in your praise reports. Each time you come out of a conversation a winner or make an advancement in your skills, jot it down. You'll see just how far you are coming in your journey!

Remember, I was the world's worst communicator. I hated to hear myself talk and I wasn't alone. I wasn't interesting. I wasn't listening. I was quiet and had absolutely no charisma. All those have changed, though. I taught myself to create my own destiny by learning to communicate effectively. Now, I am no longer at the mercy of what life dishes out to me. I speak up. I get what I want. I relate to others. I can even share more good with others. Why? Because I can communicate; and that, my friend is something worth talking about!

*"Change will happen because you make it happen."*

- Dr. Phil

## Chapter Takeaways

1. Working your communication skills out by daily drills is the ultimate life-changing strategy to effectively speaking to people. As you advance on this list, continue to employ the things you have already learned.

2. Day one begins with positive thoughts and positive input. Each day from this day forward should as well.

3. Go through the daily steps. Do each exercise with your whole heart and it will show.

4. Keep a journal. Begin at the start of your journey so you can record your progress as you go.

5. Nothing changes until you change it. By taking your communication skills into your own hands, you can change the course of your life. Take charge and watch your life do a paradigm shift for the better

# One Last Thought

Now that you have read this book, you are going to be much more aware of your communication flaws. You will probably find yourself analyzing each and every conversation you have for quite some time. That is great; for you have some excellent tools in your tool pouch now and you know how to fix the problems that may arise.

Don't forget that the exercises in this book really work. They worked for me and they'll work for you too. You don't have to settle for a life with communication barriers. Those days are over. It's time for a fresh, new change. The time is now to implement the things you have learned between the covers of this book so that you can talk to anyone, anywhere with effective, powerful communication that will get you what you want and get you where you want to go.

Thanks again for downloading this book. I wish you all the best. I know firsthand how rewarding it is to finally conquer the communication breakdown and to build skills that will speak volumes. Good luck and may you talk your heart out with effective communication that says it all.

# Could You Help?

We'd love to hear your opinion about my book. In the world of book publishing, there are a few things more valuable than honest reviews from a wide variety of readers.

Your review will help other readers find out if this book is for them. It will also help us reach more readers by increasing the visibility of this book.

# YOUR FREE BONUS

## Download another Book for Free

I want to thank you for buying this book. Our hope is to assist you even further in your quest of developing powerful self-confidence by giving you the captivating confidence workbook for free.

Click the link below to receive it:

http://www.imreadytoshine.com/confidence-workbook

This is a very comprehensible and step-by-step quick-start guide with printable sheet that will help you build your Confidence.

In addition to getting this workbook, you will also have the opportunity to get my new books for free, and receive other valuable emails that will help you.

Again, here is the link to get your free workbook.

http://www.imreadytoshine.com/confidence-workbook

# About the Authors

## Rock H. Bankole

Helping People overcome life's challenges and difficulties, and finding opportunities to turn around their life and achieve great success and happiness is Rock's core value in life.

He took a serious interest in creating step-by-step and easy to follow self-help books that are focused on solving real life challenges and help people improve their life.

Entrepreneur, author and Investor, Rock strongly believes that every human being has a power that can drive him to achieve tremendous success.

You can Follow him here

https://www.facebook.com/RockBankole/

https://twitter.com/RockBankole

## C.J. Jerabek

C.J. Jerabek is an accomplished author with many published books. Writing from her Colorado cabin and her Texas lake house, Jerabek writes on a wide variety of subjects. She especially enjoys writing books that help people.

# Check Out My Other Books

Below you'll find some of my other popular books that are popular on Amazon and Kindle as well. Simply click on the links below to check them out. Alternatively, you can visit my author page on Amazon to see other work done by me.

**Captivating Confidence: How to Confidently Take Charge of your life:**

https://www.amazon.com/CONFIDENCE-CAPTIVATING-CONFIDENTLY-confidence-development-ebook/dp/B01I1ZABRM

If the links do not work, for whatever reason, you can simply search for these titles on the Amazon website to find them.

# Additional Resources

- "Accept Them as They Are" article in Psychology Today Rick Hanson, Ph.D., neuropsychologist

- E.F. Hutton: https://en.wikipedia.org/wiki/E._F._Hutton_%26_Co.

- Virtual Speech Coach : http://www.virtualspeechcoach.com/tag/effective-communication-statistics/

- http://time.com/2917367/5-secrets-that-will-help-you-master-conversation-skills/

- http://www.huffingtonpost.com/2013/11/20/divorce-causes-_n_4304466.html

- Lifestyle website YourTango.com

- Dale Carnegie, "How to Win Friends and Influence People"

- Leil Lowndes, "How to Talk to Anyone- 92 Little Tricks for Big Success in Relationships".

- Forbes Magazine "Untapped Power of Smiling" article by Ron Gutman

- Brett and Kate McKay "The Art of Conversation: 5 Dos and Don'ts"

- http://www.artofmanliness.com/2010/09/24/the-art-of-conversation/

- https://www.psychologytoday.com/conditions/communication-disorders "communication Disorders"

- http://www.scientificamerican.com/article/the-neuroscience-of-everybody-favorite-topic-themselves/

- "The Neuroscience of Everybody's Favorite Topic" Why do people spend so much time talking about themselves? by Adrian F. Ward

- http://www.apa.org/monitor/2012/04/rejection.aspx

- Science Watch article by Kirsten Weir for
  AMERICAN PSYCHOLOGICAL ASSOCIATION

Made in the USA
Middletown, DE
08 April 2017